Copyright © 2022 by Layla Grace

Contents

A bland diet may have many potential benefits if a person suffers from stomach problems frequently, but most doctors do not prescribe any specific bland diet for patients or children. Many people find that refraining from spicy foods can help reduce heartburn, ulcers, and nausea. Some people find that recovery from stomach symptoms is aided by consuming bland, low-fiber foods like bananas, toast, and applesauce. Even so, every person's body is unique and some people may not benefit from a bland diet at all.

A bland diet includes low fiber foods that have a soft consistency and are gentle on the digestive system. Bland diets are also known as soft diets, low residue diets, and gastrointestinal soft diets.

A doctor might recommend a bland diet for people experiencing gastrointestinal inflammation from infections, diverticulitis, or the flares of a chronic condition, such as Crohn's disease or ulcerative colitis.

People with other gastrointestinal conditions, including acid reflux and peptic ulcers, may also benefit from a bland diet.

As well as specific food recommendations, people following a bland diet may also have to eat smaller meals more frequently, eat more slowly, and avoid lying down soon after eating.

Foods to Eat

People with gastrointestinal conditions may benefit from a bland diet.

It is vital that people check their individual dietary needs with a doctor before changing their diet.

Foods in a bland diet should be soft, low fat, low fiber, and easy to digest. Also, they should not contain heavy spices, flavors, or seasoning.

People tolerate different foods to different extents. Generally, however, a bland diet works to eliminate foods likely to cause digestive issues, such as bloating, diarrhea, gas, and nausea.

Since people may already be experiencing significant symptoms, the goal is to avoid foods that could cause additional symptoms or make existing ones worse.

Recommended foods include:

- tender meats, such as fish, pork, beef, and poultry
- tofu

- broth
- smooth nut butters
- eggs
- thoroughly cooked skinless, seedless vegetables, such as potatoes, squash, and carrots
- plant-based milk alternatives, such as almond milk, walnut milk, flax milk, and coconut milk
- fruit juices, although people with acid reflux may need to avoid tomato and citrus juices
- puddings and custard
- refined grains, such as rice, white bread, Cream of Wheat, and pasta
- dairy, if a person can tolerate it
- weak black tea, green tea, and some herbal teas

Foods to Avoid

Foods in a bland diet should not be tough, high fiber, high fat, spicy, or gas-producing. Such foods include:

- tough, fatty meats and meats with casings, such as sausages
- fried foods
- legumes
- spicy, seasoned, cured, or smoked meat, including fish
- vegetables that can trigger flatulence, such as cabbage, Brussels sprouts, broccoli, cucumber, and corn
- strong cheeses, such as blue cheese
- fatty dairy, such as whipping cream
- pickles
- sauerkraut
- high sugar foods
- nuts and seeds
- whole grain cereals, breads, crackers, and pasta
- crunchy nut butter

- dried fruit
- raw vegetables
- gas-producing vegetables, including broccoli, Brussels sprouts, cabbage, onions, peppers, and cauliflower
- high fiber cereals
- fried pastries, such as donuts
- gluten, if a person cannot tolerate it

The following foods and drinks may not be high in fiber but can cause gastrointestinal irritation in some conditions, such as acid reflux:

- alcohol
- certain spices and condiments, including pepper, hot sauce, and barbecue sauce
- strong seasonings, such as garlic, horseradish, and chili pepper
- caffeinated drinks, such as tea and coffee

- citrus fruits
- tomato products

Safety of Bland Diet

A bland diet is only recommended for a short time when necessary. After a person recovers or their condition improves, their doctor will advise them to start gradually increasing the amount of fiber in their diet.

Fiber offers many health benefits, so following a bland diet for an extended period of time could adversely impact health.

Eating high fiber foods can help lower levels of low-density lipoprotein, or "bad," cholesterol, promote stable blood sugar levels, nourish gut bacteria, and help with weight management.

There have not been many scientific studies regarding the effectiveness of a bland diet.

The premise of the diet is that people avoid eating foods that cause gastrointestinal symptoms, such as gas and diarrhea. The diet also promotes eating softer, milder foods, as foods with intense flavors and odors might exacerbate symptoms such as nausea.

Because the symptoms and triggers of acid reflux vary widely, there is currently little evidence to prove that people should avoid specific foods.

Due to this lack of evidence, the American College of Gastroenterology do not routinely suggest that people with gastroesophageal reflux disease eliminate foods such as chocolate, caffeine, spicy foods, citrus fruits, and carbonated drinks. However, they do say that elimination diets could be beneficial on an individual basis.

Are there any risks

A bland diet could result in constipation, since fiber helps promote regular bowel movements. A long-term bland diet can also cause changes in a person's overall health because fiber feeds healthy gut bacteria.

Benefits of Bland Diet for Diarrhea

Here are some fantastic health benefits of choosing a bland diet

1. It Helps in Curing Bacterial Food Poisoning

A bland diet is highly efficient in treating bacterial food poisoning, as well as an upset stomach. It will help you feel better within two or three days.

2. It Provides Relief from the Morning Sickness

Morning sickness is a common phenomenon in pregnant women. It is accompanied by nausea and discomfort. A bland diet can make meals short and frequent, which will provide relief from morning sickness.

3. It can Cure Gastroenteritis

Gastroenteritis is also known as infectious diarrhea, and it occurs due to infections. Bland diet tends to stabilize the process of digestion. It helps in the treatment while enhancing the absorption as well.

4. It Makes Digestion Faster and Easier

A bland diet includes simpler foods as compared to those of a regular diet. Since the number of complex substances decreases, the metabolism becomes easier. It facilitates the breakdown of a simple meal at a faster rate.

What are the Uses of Bland Diet?

Here are some beneficial uses of a bland diet

Doctors prescribe low diet post the surgery of the digestive tract of an individual, to let the digestive tract heal with simple food, before the introduction of more difficult foods to digest.

It is beneficial for the patients who are suffering from gastrointestinal problems or any other conditions, where the most important and essential requirement is proper digestion of food.

Though dairy and milk products in a bland diet are acceptable, the milk products that consist of cocoa, excessive fats, and strongly spiced cheeses, should not be consumed. Low-fat dairy products are truly useful in soothing the irritated linings of the digestive tract.

Delicious Recipes of Bland Diet

Many delicious recipes are beneficial to have while following a bland diet. For breakfast, you can choose to eat scrambled eggs, as they are proteinaceous and have a low amount of fats. For your dessert, you can prepare a sugar-free pudding and enjoy it without fearing any digestive problem.

Here is the step by step process to make these yummy bland food recipes –

Scrambled Eggs for Breakfast

Ingredients

Four eggs (for two servings)

One-fourth cup of milk

Two tablespoons of butter

Salt and pepper, as per taste

Procedure

Take a bowl and stir the ingredients except for butter for some time.

Take a pan and heat the butter in it and pour the egg mixture. When the eggs will set, pull the eggs gently from the pan.

Pull, lift and fold the egg while cooking it. Remove the scrambled eggs from heat and serve hot.

Sugar-Free Pudding for Dessert

Ingredients

Two cups of milk

One-fourth teaspoon of salt

Half cup of milk mixed with cornstarch

A three-fourths teaspoon of vanilla extract

One-eighth teaspoon of uncut stevia

Two tablespoons of butter spread (optional)

Procedure

Heat two cups of milk in a saucepan and when it gets warm, add the mixture of milk and cornstarch in it.

Boil the mixture for some time. Stir constantly for three minutes after the boil.

Turn off the heat and add the rest of the ingredients in the saucepan. Freeze the pudding and let it cool. Serve it.

Fresh Fruit Salad

Ingredients

2 cups diced fresh pineapple

1 pound strawberries, hulled and sliced

½ pint blackberries, halved

4 ripe kiwis, peeled, halved and sliced

1 cup Lime Yogurt Fruit Salad Dressing

Directions

Combine pineapple, strawberries, blackberries and kiwi in a large bowl. Serve with yogurt dressing, if desired.

Nutrition Facts

Serving Size: 3/4 cup

Per Serving: 57 calories; protein 1g; carbohydrates 13.9g; dietary fiber 3g; sugars 9.1g; fat 0.4g; vitamin a iu 82.5IU; vitamin c 73.6mg; folate 28.3mcg; calcium 25.8mg; iron 0.5mg; magnesium 18.1mg; potassium 220.6mg; sodium 1.8mg; thiamin 0.1mg.

Leek & Potato Soup

Ingredients

2 large leeks

1 tablespoon olive oil

1 small onion, diced

1 teaspoon fresh savory or thyme, chopped

2 large baking potatoes skins on, scrubbed, and cut into a ½-inch dice

⅓ cup plain whole-milk yogurt (Greek style is best)

6 cups stock, vegetable or chicken

1½ tablespoon Italian parsley, plus more for garnish, chopped

Directions

Chop off the roots and the dark green part of the leeks. Discard the roots, and rinse the dark greens well, tie them up with a piece of twine, and set aside. Quarter the white parts of the leeks lengthwise then thinly slice. Leeks hold a lot of grit and soil, so when you''re done slicing, wash them very well! Drain, and set aside.

Heat the oil in a heavy soup pot over a medium high flame. When it starts to ripple, add the onions, white parts of the leeks, and savory: fry until the leeks and onion start to soften but not color. Mix in the potato. Cover and turn the heat down to medium, stirring occasionally, 8 to 10 minutes or until the potato begins to soften. Don't let them brown.

When the potatoes are softened slightly, turn the heat up and add the yogurt and stir constantly until any water in the yogurt has evaporated and the vegetables are covered in curds.

Add the stock, the reserved bundle of leek greens, and bring the soup to a boil. Stir well to mix everything in. Turn the heat down and cook until the potatoes can be smashed against the side of the pan with a spoon, about 10 to 15 minutes. Taste for salt.

Remove the bundle of leek greens, and blend. Bring the soup back to a simmer, add the chopped parsley cook for 1 minute, then serve. Sprinkle each bowl with more parsley and a grind of black pepper.

Perfect Thick Cut Pork Chops

Ingredients

4 thick cut pork chops

olive oil

salt

pepper

Instructions

Rub about a tablespoon of olive oil over each of your pork chops. Season all sides generously with salt. Pork needs a heavy amount of salt to bring out the flavor. Salt with a heavy hand when it comes to a thick pork chop. Season lightly with freshly ground pepper as well.

Heat an oven-safe heavy skillet over high heat. Preheat an oven to 400 degrees.

Sear the pork chops for 2 minutes on each side.

Transfer skillet immediately to the oven and cook until the internal temperature of the chop reaches 145 degrees, about 15 minutes.

Let rest 5 to 10 minutes before serving.

Chicken & Rice Soup

Ingredients

1 teaspoon olive oil

½ medium onion, chopped

4 celery ribs, diced

3 medium carrots, diced

2 teaspoons dill, fresh or dried

½ cup long-grain brown rice (or white rice, see Chef Tips)

Salt and pepper, to taste

2 pounds chicken breast on the bone, skinned

5 cups water (or broth)

Chopped parsley, to garnish (optional)

Directions

Heat the olive oil in a heavy sauce-pot over medium heat. Add the onions, celery, carrots, dill, rice, salt, and pepper. Cook, stirring occasionally, until the vegetables are tender and the onions are translucent, about 8 minutes.

Add the chicken and 4 cups of water. Bring to a boil, then cover and simmer for 1 hour, adding more water if too much evaporates.

Remove the chicken and transfer to a colander. Once cool enough to handle, shred the chicken meat off the bone and return to broth to heat through. Discard the bones. Taste the soup for seasonings, add parsley if using, and serve.

Cottage Pie

Ingredients

4 large Yukon Gold potatoes, quartered

6 tablespoons butter, divided

1 clove garlic, minced

salt and pepper to taste

1 tablespoon olive oil

1 pound lean ground beef

1 tablespoon herbes de Provence

1 teaspoon ground nutmeg

1 ½ cups frozen peas

Directions

Preheat oven to 350 degrees F (175 degrees C). Lightly grease a 9 inch deep-dish pie plate.

Place potatoes into a pot; cover with salted water, and bring to a boil over high heat. Reduce heat to medium-low, cover; simmer until tender, about 20 minutes. Drain; mash with 2 tablespoons of the butter and the garlic. Season to taste with salt and pepper; set aside.

Meanwhile, heat the olive oil in a skillet over medium heat. Add ground beef, herbes de Provence, and nutmeg; cook and stir until beef is lightly brown and crumbly, about 10 minutes. Spread the beef evenly in the prepared pie plate. Cover evenly with the peas; spread the mashed potatoes over the peas. Dot the casserole with the remaining butter.

Bake, uncovered, in the preheated oven until heated through and bubbly, about 20 minutes.

Easy Baked Salmon with Garlic Butter

Ingredients

4 tablespoon unsalted butter (melted)

2 cloves fresh garlic (minced)

Handful of fresh parsley (finely chopped)

Salt and pepper to taste

3 tablespoon freshly squeezed lemon juice

4 salmon fillets (any size or weight will work for this recipe)

Instructions

Preheat your oven to 400F (200°C). Line a baking tray with tin foil.

Clean the salmon and remove any visible bones. If the skin is still on, pat it dry.

In a small bowl, mix together the melted butter, garlic, lemon juice, salt, and pepper until well-combined.

Add the salmon fillets to the baking tray, skin-side down. Brush with the garlic butter until well-covered, but reserve some to brush on the fish after it's done baking.

Place in the oven and bake for 12 – 18 minutes depending on the thickness of the salmon fillets. I find that 15 minutes is usually the right amount of time.

Take the salmon out of the oven. If baked with the skin, remove that now. Brush the fillets with another layer of garlic butter, then drizzle with fresh lemon juice and top with chopped parsley.

White Pizza

Ingredients

4 cups spinach

2 cups Greek yogurt

5 sprigs rosemary, chopped

¼ cup fresh oregano, chopped

3 tablespoons garlic, chopped

Salt and pepper to taste

2 tablespoons cornmeal or semolina flour

1 recipe Pizza Dough or store-bought

1 ½ cup fresh mozzarella, diced

¼ cup olive oil

Directions

Preheat oven to 400 degrees

In a small pot of boiling water, cook the spinach for about a minute or until it wilts and turns bright green. Shock in ice water

In a medium bowl, whisk together yogurt, rosemary, oregano, and garlic, season with salt and pepper.

Sprinkle cornmeal or semolina flour on 2 baking sheets.

Portion and shape pizza dough and place on floured pans. Spread an even layer of the yogurt sauce on each of the pizzas. Top with cooked spinach and mozzarella cheese. Drizzle with olive oil.

Bake until the crust and bottom of the pizzas is golden brown, about 15 minutes.

Simple Kitchari

Ingredients

¼ cup split mung beans (these can be found at most natural food stores or online. They can also be found whole rather than split, you can use these but be sure to increase your cooking time to break them down fully)

½ cup organic basmati rice

1 3x2 inch strip of kombu, cut into small pieces

6-8 cups of filtered water

3-4 cups fresh, organic and seasonal veggies (use at least one green veggie such as spinach or kale and one orange or root vegetable such as carrot, sweet potato or squash)

1-2 Tbsp of CCF blend (made by grinding equal parts of cumin, coriander and fennel seed or by mixing the pre-ground spices)

⅛ tsp asafoetida

½ - 1 tsp turmeric powder

1 Tbsp chopped fresh ginger root

¼ - ½ cup shredded coconut

1 cup loosely packed chopped, fresh organic cilantro

2-3 Tbsp ghee (Vegans can use coconut oil in the warmer months or sesame oil in the cooler months use less ghee if you have kapha imbalance, lots of accumulation, or excess weight).

1 tsp rock salt

Instructions

Rinse the rice and split mung beans (I don't really measure I just do a 2:1 ratio of rice to beans) then put them in a pressure cooker with the kombu and water enough to cover by at least an inch or 2 (about 3 cups of water depending on your pot).

Boil until soft, 10-15 minutes (longer if not using pressure cooker). Chop veggies and cilantro and grind spices (if using whole spices) as the rice and beans cook.

Add the veggies (keep kale or quick-cooking veggies out for now), add 2 more cups of water and cover. Cook 3-5 minutes or so until the water boils veggies are starting to soften. Add more water and adjust temperature as needed.

Once veggies start to soften, add the diced ginger, coconut and spices (cumin, coriander, fennel, asafoetida and turmeric). When making a warming kitchari in the fall or winter I'll add a little black pepper and a dash of cinnamon too, maybe some raisins.

Add the kale, spinach or other quick- cooking veggies and the fresh cilantro. Stir.

Then add ghee and rock salt.

Turn off heat, and serve with fresh cilantro and coconut garnish and a wedge of lime if you like.

Vegetable Soup Diet Recipe

Ingredients

8 cups low sodium vegetable broth

3 cups broccoli florets

2 cups cauliflower florets

2 medium zucchini sliced

1 large red onion diced

2 14.5 oz canned diced tomatoes, in juice

4 cloves garlic minced

2 large carrots peeled & diced

1 large red bell pepper

1 large green bell pepper

3 tbsp tomato paste

2 bay leaves fresh or dry

2 tsp Italian seasoning

Instructions

In a large pot drizzle in the olive oil, and turn the heat to medium

Once the oil is nice & hot, add in the onions and cook for 2 minutes.

Add in the garlic, and cook for about 1 more minute.

Add in the carrots, and bell peppers. Stir and cook for 3 minutes.

Now add in the tomato paste, and pour in the tomatoes with juice, and broth.

Stir the ingredients, then add in the bay leaves and seasonings.

Simmer for 8 - 10 minutes.

Toss in the broccoli, cauliflower, and zucchini.

Simmer until tender.

Fish out the bay leaves.

Serve & enjoy!

Mango Salsa

1 large peeled, pitted and chopped mango

1/3 cup chopped red bell pepper

1/4 cup minced red onion

1/2 tablespoon chopped fresh cilantro

1/2 tablespoon lime juice

1/8 teaspoon salt

Instructions

In a small bowl, stir together all ingredients for mango salsa.

Cook chicken on a lightly oiled grill over medium heat for about 5 minutes on each side or until lightly charred and cooked through. Let cool slightly and cut into bite-size strips. (You may substitute leftover grilled chicken.)

Puree the tomato sauce and dried pepper in a blender or food processor. Transfer to a small saucepan and simmer over medium heat for 15 minutes. Add grilled chicken to pan and toss well to coat; season to taste with salt. Place flour tortillas on a flat surface.

Top half of each tortilla with equal amounts of cheese, mango, bell pepper, green onion and chicken; fold over tortilla. Cook in a large skillet on both sides until cheese is melted and tortilla is crisp, about 5 minutes on each side. Serve with mango salsa.

Makes 4 entree servings, or 8 appetizer servings.

Nutrition Information Per Entree Serving:

560 calories 30 g protein 64 g carbohydrates

19 g total fat (10 g. saturated) 78 mg cholesterol

1,380 mg sodium 6 g fiber

Salsa Stoup

Ingredients

1 green pepper (chopped)

1 onion (chopped)

3 ribs of celery (chopped)

28 ounce can stewed tomatoes

1 can crushed tomatoes

1 can chicken broth

Procedure

In a big pot, sautç the peppers, onion, and celery until soft, then add everything else (both cans of tomatoes and the chicken broth), and bring to a boil.

Chicken Stir Fry

Ingredients

Chicken (chopped up)

Frozen/Fresh chopped up vegetables - you can use whatever you have on hand

Soy sauce

Hot sauce

Procedure

In a stir fry pan or regular frying pan, cook vegetables 'til soft, then add chicken and cook it until it is done all the way through, then add as much soy/hot sauce as you want until it looks good to you. Can be eaten by itself or served over rice/noodles or whatever.

Steak & Veggies

Ingredients

Hamburger (as lean as possible)

Mixed frozen vegetables (corn, peas, carrots)

A1 steak sauce

Procedure

In a stir fry pan or regular frying pan, cook vegetables until they are thawed, then add hamburger and cook until brown. Then during the last minute of cooking, add a good amount of A1 to the pan and cook it. This will thicken the steak sauce and have it stick to the vegetables and meat. Then serve and eat.

Tuna Patties

Ingredients

Canned tuna

1 egg white for each can of tuna

Some oatmeal for texture

Vegetables: onions and peppers

Fat free cheese

Hot sauce

Procedure

Mix all the above ingredients in a bowl. Then form into patties. Pan fry each side until golden brown, using fat free cooking spray in the pan. It's that easy. This is a good recipe because you can add whatever you want after the tuna, egg white, and oatmeal. Put in whatever vegetables and flavors that you personally like.

Protein Bars

Ingredients

4 oz Sugar Free/Fat Free Jell-O or similar (Butterscotch)

8 oz cottage cheese

3 cups oatmeal (old-fashioned oatmeal)

1/2 cup milk

1.5 scoop casein

2 scoops whey (chocolate)

2 tbsp peanut butter

Directions

It couldn't be easier to make these, just mix them in a bowl, spread out on a tray, and leave it in the refrigerator overnight. In the morning, cut into squares, and eat when you're on the go!

The remaining recipes are still fairly simple to make, and taste great. I prefer to make in portions to last me at least two days, so I don't have to cook every night.

Pineapple Curry

Ingredients

1 small can of pineapple, cubed

.5 tsp curry powder

chili powder to taste

Directions

Simply combine all the ingredients with enough water to cover the chicken, and boil at a low heat setting for 25-30 minutes. Very easy and tasty, tender meats work best.

Fried Rice

Ingredients

2 eggs, yolk & white

Worcestershire sauce

Soy sauce (low sodium preferred)

Vegetables to stir fry with

Cooking oil

Directions

Cook the rice separately. Using basmati rice, I bring the rice to a boil (1:1.5 of rice: water), cover and cook at medium-low heat for 10 minutes. Fluff/Dry the rice somewhat.

Heat the cooking oil in a pan. If you are going to add meat (chicken, etc), cook the meat in this oil, and set aside on another plate. No needs to wipe down the pan really, scramble the eggs in it, and chop finely with a spatula (or similar implement). Add vegetables and rice, and add Worcestershire & soy, in equal portions (1:1). Cook until the vegetables are ready, turning occasionally so the rice doesn't burn. Mix with meat if desired, and presto, food.

Curry:

2 - 2.5 lbs beef, chicken, or lamb

1 tbsp garam marsala

1 tsp ground cumin

1 medium onion (diced)

1.5 tsp curry powder (dry)

.75 - 1 cup water (depends on how much meat you have)

1 tbsp lemon juice (optional)

.5 tsp chili powder

Crock pot, or equivalent

2 tbsp whole wheat flour (optional - used to thicken sauce)

Directions

Cube the meat of choice. If you're using beef, broiling steaks work well, and are easy to work with. Lamb is also good, and while more expensive tends to be a more tender meat, and makes for a great curry.

Dice onion, and place in crock pot. Add cubed beef, cumin, curry powder, garam marsala, lemon juice, chili powder.

Add .75 - 1 cup of water, depending on how much meat you used. The water line should rise to be approximately as high as the meat being used, it's not necessary to completely immerse the meat with water.

(in a crock pot, or similar) cook on low for 8 hours, or if you're in a hurry, cook on high for 4-5 hours. Cooking it slowly will give a much more tender meat, and is my preference for making curry. If you are using a pot, set the meat to a simmer, and cook for 2 - 2.5 hours (approximately).

Pad Thai With Chicken

Worcestershire sauce

Soy sauce

Pad Thai

Chicken

Olive oil

Sesame oil

Chili powder (to taste)

Teriyaki marinade

Broccoli - finely chopped

Carrots - finely chopped

2 Eggs

Pad Thai is rice noodles, which has the ingredients of rice, and water (jasmine rice for mine). It is very cheap, easy to work with, and can usually be found in supermarkets (often listed as one of the 'Asian Foods').

Directions:

Marinade 6-8 oz chicken (cubed) in 1 tbsp teriyaki, 1 tbsp Worcestershire, 1 tsp sesame oil, and chili powder to taste. I usually aim for at least 3 hours, sometimes I do it overnight.

Place Pad Thai in a pot with lukewarm water. Allow to soak for 45-60 minutes. This will soften the noodles to an 'al dente' texture - strain the noodles, and place aside.

Alternatively, cooking in boiling water for 2-3 minutes will prepare them.

Scramble 2 eggs in a bowl, set aside.

In a large skillet, fry the teriyaki chicken until cooked thoroughly. Empty into the bowl you will use for eating. No need to wipe down the pan after this.

Cook the eggs in the skillet - the egg will absorb most of the leftover sauce from frying the chicken. Chop with spatula until fine, and add finely chopped broccoli/carrots (keep egg in pan). Continue frying until broccoli is finished.

Add Pad Thai into the mixture, and use about a 50/50 split of Worcestershire/soy to add flavoring to the mixture. Toss everything together in the skillet and fry for a few minutes (don't let it sit there - the Pad Thai will dry out).

Lasagna

Ingredients

Tomato sauce

Basil

Thyme

Oregano

10-12 oz tuna fish

6-8 oz chicken breast (cubed)

Ricotta cheese/cottage cheese, 10-15 oz

Low fat cheddar/monterey jack cheese (optional, depending how strict you are)

Lasagna noodles (cooked)

It's Easy To Make:

In a oven-safe tray, cover the bottom with tomato sauce, spiced with some basil/thyme/oregano.

Add a layer of cooked lasagna on top of the tomato sauce. Cover top with a thin layer of chicken and tuna fish.

Add some ricotta cheese or cottage cheese (I prefer to use ricotta) on top. No need to cover all over the lasagna - it will spread out just fine.

Sprinkle cheese on top (if desired).

Repeat steps 1-4 for as many layers as desired (I generally use 3 layers.)

Cover, and heat at 375 (Fahrenheit!) for 35 minutes, then remove the cover and cook for another 10 minutes.

Peanut Butter Oatmeal

A nuttier and creamier oatmeal that is easy to prepare.

Instruction

Prepare 1/2 cup of instant or old-fashioned oatmeal according to directions using 1/2 cup of lowfat or skim milk. Add a tablespoon of peanut butter, smooth or crunchy style depending on preference. After mixing, An additional scoop of protein powder of any flavor can also be added. Pour in additional milk or water to obtain the desired consistency and temperature. Stir well and enjoy.

Washington State Mashed Potatoes With Roasted Garlic

Ingredients

2 lbs Washington russet potatoes, peeled and quartered

1/4 cup milk

2 tbsp mayonnaise

1 tbsp butter or margarine

1/2 tsp salt

1/4 tsp white pepper

1 whole medium head garlic

Makes 6 servings

Instructions

Bake garlic at 375 Â°F 45 minutes. Cut top 1/2 inch off head, squeeze to remove pulp and mash. Boil potatoes about 30 minutes or until tender. Drain well. In a mixing bowl, combine hot potatoes, milk, mayonnaise, butter, salt and pepper. Whip at low speed only until smooth. Add garlic and mix well.

Nutrition Facts

Calories 171 Protein 4.4 g Carbohydrates 28.9 g Fat 6 g Cholesterol 9 mg Dietary fiber 3.5 g Sodium 248 mg

Crunchy Tuna Rice Salad

Ingredients

3 cups cooked rice, cooled

1 12-ounce can water packed tuna, drained and flaked

2 medium carrots, shredded

1 medium-size green or red bell pepper, chopped

1 cup chopped jicama

3/4 cup thinly sliced green onions

1-1/2 cups nonfat plain yogurt

1 teaspoon lemon pepper

1/4 teaspoon salt

1/4 teaspoon ground black pepper

3 whole pita bread rounds, halved

Shredded lettuce

Instructions

Combine rice, tuna, carrots, bell pepper, jicama and onion in large bowl. Add yogurt, lemon pepper, salt and pepper. Toss to combine ingredients. Chill at least 1 hour. Serve in pita bread with lettuce.

Makes 6 servings.

Substitute 1 (6-ounce) can water chestnuts, drained and chopped, for the jicama if desired.

Nutrition Facts

Each Serving Provides: 288 calories

20 g. protein 1 g. fat 47 g. carbohydrate 4 g. dietary fiber 15 mg. cholesterol 508 mg. sodium

Is Bland Diet Safe for Kids?

The bland food diet is often useful for children who suffer from an upset stomach or diarrhea. It provides rest to the digestive tract and reduces the amount of stool produced.

Though it serves great benefits to most of the age groups, according to the experts, a bland diet might not go well for sick children as the bland diet foods have low fiber and lack enough nutrition which might not fulfill the nutrient requirements of children at their growing stages.

According to pediatrics, the diet for children must include enough fruits and vegetables, complex carbohydrates, meat, and yogurt.

Bland diet for diarrhea and other gut-related problems is highly effective and beneficial. Since it simplifies the complexity of digestion, it provides relief from various digestive issues.

The recipes of the bland diet are quite comfortable and nutritious. Most importantly, they save a lot of time while preparing the dishes. The benefits of bland food are countless, and it puts our health on the right track.

1. What is a Bland Diet?

A bland diet is a planned diet that helps in effectively curing the discomfort caused by gastric and intestinal problems. It is also helpful in treating various disorders related to the gut.

2: What are Bland Foods?

Bland foods are the food items that constitute to form a bland diet collectively. Bland foods have low fiber content and less amount of fats. The aim is to make the process of digestion easy.

3: What Can You Eat on a Bland Diet?

If you are following a bland diet, then you have plenty of options having low fiber and less fat to eat. One must avoid sugary food items too. It also includes low-fat dairy products.

How can you make a bland diet appealing?

The enjoyment of eating food is related to that food's flavor, temperature, aroma, texture, and presentation. Making modifications to any of these attributes may often make a food more suitable to an individual's appetite. While the next section will go over some of the changes that can be made to the actual food itself, this section contains advice regarding the presentation of the food.

The Sensory Aspects of Appetite:

The smell of food plays an important role in stimulating appetite. The nerve receptors in the nose send signals to the brain, which then sends signals to other glands which release appetite related hormones. In the end, people feel more hungry after smelling the aroma of food. Basically, try to make sure foods have a pleasant smell before eaten. Some herbs and spices, which we will see in the next section, can help improve the smell of foods.

Food temperature can also influence its desirability. Typically, foods that aid us in maintaining a pleasant body temperature are appealing. For example, warm soup in the cold winter, and cold drinks in the summer or after exercise are common.

General temperature preferences differ from person to person, but everyone should make sure to eat food at the temperature they are most familiar and comfortable with in order to increase the appeal of it.

Appetite is also affected by colors. The most accepted colors for edible food are brown, red, and green. Blue has been found to be an appetite suppressant, possibly because our nature tells us to avoid darker colors due to a greater potential to be poisonous.

Serving the food on a light-colored plate may make the meal appear to be more fresh and thus more appealing. As we know, many of us tend to "eat with our eyes," so incorporating a good variety of colors in a bland dish may be enough to trick us into enjoying the meal more.

There are also social aspects of eating. Many find their dining experiences more enjoyable when they share it with other people, allowing for interesting conversations, jokes, and stories. Eating with others may help with taking the mind off of food that is not particularly appealing. Just make sure not to allow others to compromise a diet.

Some degree of enjoyment can also be attributed to how the food feels, its texture. Obviously, not many would prefer to eat something that would feel like sand. The dryness of a food is something that can be directly changed to meet one's preferences.

The way in which foods are eaten also fall into the sense of touch category. Preparing food meant to be eaten with the hands instead of utensils might be a fun change for some.

Lastly, eating simple and plain foods in a dull place obviously does not help it to be any less bland. Try eating in a different environment for a change. Have a picnic outdoors, or go to a nice restaurant if nutritional information is readily available.

Varietal Tips:

Many of the foods that plague the bland diet often come in different varieties and flavors. Maintaining a good selection to choose from often helps alleviate some of the tedium and boredom associated with bland diets. The following are some examples of common foods that have much room for variation.

Oatmeal: comes in different varieties- instant, old fashioned, and steel cut oats all offer different texture experiences. The instant oatmeal is also available in many different flavors, allowing the dieter a greater degree of convenience. Note that the flavored oatmeal comes at the price of containing some sugar, but it's usually not enough to worry over.

Protein Powders: many people, bodybuilders in particular, choose to supplement with protein. They often come in many flavors to accommodate differing tastes.

Rice: there are different varieties of rice- brown rice, white rice, wild rice, as well as short, medium, and long grains, giving different textures and tastes.

Potatoes: Russet Burbank, Yellow Finn, and Red Gold potatoes are different types. The good thing about potatoes is that they can be prepared in many different ways. They can be served baked, boiled, and mashed among other possibilities in order to make them more appealing to the diner.

Water: there are many flavored waters available that are still calories free.

Tuna: there is a variety of different species. It can be purchased in "solid" or "chunk" forms and packed in either water or oil to suit personal texture and consistency preferences.

Yogurt: is often made in many different flavors and consistencies, some even with real fruits.

Eating Alternately:

Another strategy is to prepare meals that consist of a combination of differing foods eaten separately, but alternately. Many "bland" dieters may eat foods separately, but not alternately. As an example, the following bland meal of plain lettuce, plain chicken breast, and plain baked potato, may be eaten systematically, one by one, since the diner knows each one is not very appealing by itself anyway.

However, the body can be tricked into finding the foods more appealing if the foods are eaten in an alternating fashion, eating some from each food a little at a time. Using this eating method keeps the taste buds guessing and may make the meal more enjoyable.

Additions:

What types of additions or spices can be used?

It turns out that variety is not only the figurative spice of life, but also food, as we saw. However, there are also real spices, herbs, and other additions that can be used to make food more appealing. These additions can work to enhance flavor, aroma, texture, and color of food.

The following additives work to improve some of these aspects which we now know are essential for the enjoyment of food.

MSG (monosodium glutamate): a flavor enhancing substance that can be added before or during cooking to improve the savory taste of foods. The benefits of this additive are that it does not affect metabolism and that it can reduce the amount of regular salt used while still improving taste.

In general, the FDA ruled that it is safe for consumption and had no relation to long-term adverse affects. However, just so you are aware, there are some cases of unpleasant, short-term side effects in some individuals.

Bouillon Cubes: these come in a wide array of flavors and enhance both the flavor and aroma of a food.

Tabasco/Hot Sauces: for those that like hot and spicy dishes, this is the perfect ingredient.

Ketchup: a popular condiment to improve flavor and gives the food more color. It is mainly made of tomatoes, but there are other ingredients as well--watch out for excessive salt and sugar content. In general, though, ketchup is a good low-calorie addition.

Mustard: another common condiment that tends to have a sharp flavor while enhancing the color of a dish. It is prepared from mustard seeds and other ingredients, so be sure to check out the salt and sugar content again, but in most cases mustard tends to be a low-calorie choice.

Pickles/Relish: this is a good pick for adding a more sweet or salty taste, while possibly adding some crunchiness to a food. There are many varieties available, but the main things to look for are the salt and sugar content, which may not be desirable for some.

Soy Sauce: adds a salty, slightly sweet flavor. It can be used as a dipping sauce or added directly to food to add its color and flavor improvements. The downside to soy sauce is that even the light versions contain a good deal of sodium.

Lettuce: a flexible vegetable that can be easily added to many dishes or on sandwiches to give it a more fresh feel and crunchy texture. There is really no downside to lettuce since it is basically a calorie-less fiber, which will only aid the body's digestive system.

Horseradish/Wasabi: adds a strong flavor that can also produce a slight burning sensation in the sinus cavity instead of on the tongue itself. These are generally low in calories and added in small amounts. My recommendation is to use some on sandwiches.

Sauerkraut: made by fermenting cabbage. It is distinguished by its sour and salty flavor. It's commonly added to meat dishes, but I also like it on sandwiches and with potatoes. The only thing to worry about with sauerkraut is that it does contain a moderate amount of salt.

Steak Sauces: has a peppery taste that can be sweet or tart. Can be put over meat to enhance taste at the cost of adding some salt. Some sauces may also have moderate sugar content, so be sure to check if necessary.

Barbecue Sauces: are marked by their combination of sour, sweet, and spicy tastes. They are really good to use over meats during or after cooking, or as a dipping sauce. The main drawback of this condiment is that they typically contain a moderate amount of sugar.

Mayonnaise: an emulsion and popular sandwich spread which may improve taste and give a more oily and moist texture. The problem that most people have with mayonnaise is that it also adds many fat calories, and should be used sparingly, if at all, when this is a concern.

Salsa: these are usually based on tomatoes and other vegetables. They help make food look brighter in color and spicier in flavor. They do contain some sodium to be aware of, but are good to use in dishes that involve tortilla wraps.

Salad Dressings: eating vegetables and salads plain is probably the ultimate bland food. Fortunately, there are plenty of low-calorie and low-sodium dressing available for all the non-masochists out there.

Salt: pure salt can be used as a seasoning for just about everything. It generally makes bland foods more palatable. Salt is also an additive in bread dough as an aid to making sure the texture and consistency turns out correctly after baking. Humans have been shown to be able to tolerate a wide range of sodium intake, but it is also shown that average blood pressure levels also tend to rise with increased intake.

For those with high blood pressure, using salt as an additive may present an issue, but for others the main drawback is that it may promote some undesired water retention.

Pepper: often found sitting right beside the salt and adds a spicy heat. Black pepper, especially, is actually very healthy. It not only adds flavor, but also helps the body absorb the nutrients in the food we eat.

Garnishes: lemon wedges, parsley, orange slices, and chives among other fruits/vegetables can be placed on or alongside the food to add color and attractiveness.

Cinnamon: a common spice with a pleasant aroma and flavor. It's a perfect addition to a bowl of oatmeal.

Ginger, onion powder, garlic, chili powder, curry powder are all other good seasonings to add while cooking food to improve flavor as well as scent.

Thyme, oregano, paprika, nutmeg, mint, basil, and marjoram are all common herbs used in cooking to enhance flavor.

The following herbs, which tend to be more bitter, have been shown to have a relation with increasing a person's appetite: gentian, bitter orange, cinnamon, coriander, dandelion, hops, horehound, rosemary, wormwood, and yarrow.

Artificial Sweeteners: these are non-carbohydrate substances that taste sweet. While they do not add calories, the body may react to them in ways similar to sugar since the body perceives it as sweet. The result may be increased saliva and insulin output.

We know insulin is an appetite-stimulating hormone, so using these artificial sweeteners may actually make one more hungry in the long run. Splenda, aspartame, and saccharin are examples of such sweeteners. While they may make bland food more appealing, there is also ongoing controversy about these substances and their role in certain health issues, so it may be best to use these sparingly and at your own risk.

Often the best way to find out which additives suit individual preferences is just to experiment. Feel free to try various combinations of the seasonings and condiments as well. There's bound to be a way to make any bland food more appetizing.

How can you make a bland diet appealing?

The name of the game is imagination. There are plenty of condiments at your disposal, and used correctly, add a world of flavor without a lot in extra calories. Which sounds better: a plain chicken breast, plain brown rice, and a steamed carrot, or alternatively, peanut chicken served with stir-fried rice, with vegetables and a couple eggs in the mix?

Chicken:

The staple of practically every bodybuilder's diet, chicken breast can be either a pleasant treat or a nightmare to eat. It really takes very little to make it into a good tasting meat. My preferred way to spice things up is to marinade chicken, although there are many other options available.

 Tuna:

Love it or hate it, there's no way around it. Tuna fish is a cheap source of protein. However, many don't like the taste of it, so there are several options to change the flavor. One way is actually to simply rinse the tuna fish using a strainer. Odd as it sounds, it will 'remove' the taste normally associated with tuna fish, however may leave it a bit dry.

With tuna, lime and lemon juices work very well to mask the bland flavor, although I prefer to just incorporate it in my cooking. It tastes much better when incorporated into a meal, while providing all the same nutritional value. Tuna lasagna anyone?

Rice:

I've grown up on rice, simply put. It's just been a staple in my diet since I was a young child, so it feels normal to me to eat it daily (in fact, it feels odd when I don't have rice!). However, rice tends not to be the most flavorful. How to dress it up a bit? Here are a few ideas:

Cook the rice in a chicken or beef broth (bouillon) to add a bit of flavor. This is a great low calorie way to enhance the taste of rice. Alternatively, when cooking the meat for dinner (such as chicken), boil it in water with barbeque sauce mixed in, and when done use the remaining liquid as a sauce for the rice. This makes a quick, easy way to flavor the rice a bit further.

Vegetables:

Steamed vegetables can be very drab, especially for those of us who really just don't like vegetables. Instead of trying to shovel down vegetables, make them in a more pleasant fashion. Make a stir-fry from the vegetables you're going to be eating, and mix with the rice. I use a mixture of soy/Worcestershire sauce when doing the stir-fry, and makes eating my vegetables not just easier, but pleasant!

Additions:

What types of additions or spices can be used?

Worcestershire Sauce:

That's right; it's not just for burgers anymore. Worcestershire sauce makes an excellent base for marinades, because it has a very robust flavor. Additionally, Worcestershire has much less sodium than soy sauce does, and makes an excellent substitute for it (especially in low-sodium diets!).

Chili Powder:

It is amazing what a bit of chili powder can do for meats. Depending on the power of the chili powder, and a person's individual tolerance that determines how much would be used. Chili powder also happens to be a mild thermogenic, as an added bonus.

Low Sodium Soy Sauce:

This is an excellent substitute for those who enjoy soy sauce (and who doesn't, in a good stir fry?), however regular soy sauce is loaded with sodium. While useful in cooking, I often still prefer to use Worcestershire, as I prefer the flavor of it.

Peanut Butter:

As odd as it may sound, natural peanut butter is excellent for making marinades, and for brushing on meats. Given that natural peanut butter only contains ground peanuts and some salt, it becomes great for cooking with. Peanuts happen to be a very good source of monounsaturated fat, which only furthers the benefit of cooking with peanut butter.

Sugar-Free Barbeque (BBQ) Sauce:

Useful not only during a barbeque, BBQ sauce makes for an excellent marinade, and is a quick and easy way to make good tasting meat.

McCormick Spices:

McCormick makes a large range of spices for meats, my favorite being the 'Montreal Chicken' seasoning. This works very well not only with chicken, but with other meats in general. It only takes a little bit too properly flavor meat. I use about a fourth of a teaspoon with these spices, generally speaking.

Curry Powder:

Excellent for making quick curried meat, the leftover liquid from making the curry is a good sauce for use on rice or potatoes, enhancing the flavor.

Cumin:

It is easy to go overboard with cumin, as it has a rather overpowering taste! Just a bit of cumin is all that is necessary, to give a more robust taste. This spice is very popular to use in Indian and Middle Eastern cooking.

Bouillon:

Typically, bouillon can be found in small cubes at the local supermarket. It is sometimes referred to as "stock," and makes a great broth for simmering. One of my favorite ways to use them is to use bouillon when making rice. Instead of cooking the rice in just plain water, cook it in water with bouillon.

Of course, I have only gone through a small fraction of what is available. Even juices from fruits make great marinades, such as the juice of oranges and especially limes.

Experimentation is the key to success with cooking, not every dish prepared will be a smash hit (if you'd had my roommate's cooking, there would be no doubt this is true!).

Conclusion

A soft, bland diet may benefit people whose gastrointestinal systems are compromised and need time to heal. Foods in a bland diet should be easy to digest and unlikely to cause additional pain or symptoms.

A bland diet can be used to treat ulcers, heartburn, nausea, vomiting and gas. You may also need to eat bland foods after stomach or intestinal surgery.

A bland diet is made up of foods that are soft, not very spicy, and low in fiber. If you're on a bland diet, you shouldn't eat spicy, fried, or raw foods. Avoid alcohol or caffeinated drinks.

Your doctor or nurse will tell you when you can start eating other foods again. It is still important to eat healthy foods when you add foods back in. Your doctor can refer you to a dietitian or nutritionist to help you plan a healthy diet.

The goal of a bland diet is to give the digestive system a rest. Foods with fiber are harder for the body to break down, so people following a bland diet tend to avoid foods that contain fiber.

For people experiencing a flare of Crohn's disease or ulcerative colitis, a bland, low fiber diet may help reduce the number and size of bowel movements.

For people with gastrointestinal irritation, eliminating foods that create stomach acid can help prevent further irritation.

Surgeons may recommend that people preparing for surgery or a medical procedure involving the digestive system should also adopt a bland or soft diet.

Some research suggests that various forms of fasting may be helpful for digestive conditions, because they can promote intestinal cell regeneration and give the bowel a complete rest.

www.ingramcontent.com/pod-product-compliance
Lightning Source LLC
Chambersburg PA
CBHW052203150726
48002CB00003B/1096